Contents

D0549500

Introduction
Technology

Glittering, gleaming and winking at you from all angles, technology is everywhere. Just take a look – nearly every man-made thing you see is an invention! Usually designed to solve a problem or make a task easier, technology can also help you have fun. Always looking to the future, it uses science to make more useful materials and better, more efficient machines.

The great granddaddy of all inventors was the ancient Greek brainbox Archimedes (c. 287–212 BCE), the original gadget geek. (No doubt, he'd be bitterly disappointed to read this, because he always fancied himself as a top mathematician.) But, he just couldn't stop inventing great gizmos. The Archimedes' screw is still used today to lift water and is the guiding principle behind a ship's propeller. His "death ray" used mirrors to concentrate the Sun's energy onto Roman ships, while a giant claw tipped them over backwards! Once upon a time the cutting edge of high-tech was a chariot or a boat made of grass. But who knows what's coming next – hover shoes, self-cleaning clothes, remote-controlled rain?

Archimedes

Chapter 1
Movers 'n' Shakers

Some of these mini marvels have been around a very long time, and with good reason. Each one is a regular superhero, saving you work by swinging mechanical advantage your way. These guys allow you to shift a heavy load over a short distance with little effort. So what's their secret? It lies in transforming a low-force, long-distance input into a high-force, short-distance output. That's how diddy Screw and Lever manage to lift a car in a screw jack. It's time to find out how these pint-sized heroes operate (no mechanical contraption could work without them). Ready to let them loose?

Wheel
and Axle

Gears

Screw

Rack and
Pinion

Bearing

Lever

Pulley

Hydraulics

Spring

Control System

Wheel and Axle
Movers 'n' Shakers

* Circular wheel is connected to machinery by rod-like axle
* Together they make possible the forward motion of vehicles
* Rolling is easier than sliding, so force required to move is less

Hey there, let's start this thing a-rollin'! We are the winning combo that really gets people on the move. Rickshaws and racers, scooters and skateboards – anything that uses a disc shape to trundle along sets our unique skills in motion. We're a "wheely" good invention!

Just imagine how important simple rollers are for factory conveyor belts, postal sorting offices, travelators and luggage carousels. Sure, Wheel does all the work, but it would be useless without sturdy Axle connecting that dizzy disc to the mechanism. Most axles sit dead-centre, allowing Wheel to spin freely. Placed off-centre, though, Axle makes a special device called a cam, which has an up-and-down element to its movement. Think wobbly drag-along toy and you've got it. Rock 'n' roll!

● First wheel-and-axle combination: c.3500 BCE (chariot)
● Wheel-and-axle applications: waterwheel, doorknob, rotary whisk, fishing reel
● World's first Ferris Wheel: 1893 (Chicago World's Fair, USA)

Wheel and Axle

Gears

☀ Transmit motion from one part of a machine to another
☀ When engaged, turning one gear causes the next to rotate
☀ Change speed and create mechanical advantage

All "geared" up, we are characters with real drive. We transfer energy from power source to wheel. We run like clockwork. Once we're on a roll, there's no stopping us!

You may be familiar with the cog – a wheel with straight teeth around its outer edge – but there are also bevel gears (where slanting teeth transfer motion around a corner) and worm gears (shafts with a screw thread). We're "engaging" fellows and love to mesh with others of our kind. A small gear driving a larger one needs to rotate many times to get the larger one to turn once. This slows the motion but also requires less force to drive. (Car transmission works like this.) Mechanical timepieces use us in exacting combos to drive both their hands accurately at different speeds. We've got the gear!

● Transmission: two or more gears operating together
● Gear ratio: relationship between the number of times connected gears rotate
● World's longest two-wheeled bicycle: 28.1 m

Gears

Screw

✳ An axle with a sloped spiral track called a thread
✳ The thread converts rotary motion to linear motion
✳ Works with a gear to turn direction of rotation through 90°

I'm totally screwy! Whirling and twirling, I'm a clever little device made from a sloping surface that winds around a cylinder. Wrap a right-angled triangle made from paper around a pencil and you'll see exactly how I turn.

As I rotate, my sloped thread transfers circular motion to horizontal motion. In doing so, it reduces the distance travelled for the same effort, bringing more forceful drive. With every glorious twist, I move forward and this allows my thread to bite and worm its way easily into wood. I'm best known for the short, sharp, metal spikes that fix one thing to another, but look about and you'll find me in screw-top lids and twist-fasteners, in propeller blades, cooling fans and corkscrews. Once you start looking, you'll find my spiralling forms utterly mesmerizing!

● World's first screw: 3rd century BCE (Archimedes' screw, ancient Greece)
● First screw-cutting lathe: 1770 (Jess Ramsden, UK)
● Invention of the Phillips head screw: 1930s (Henry Phillips, USA)

Screw

Rack and Pinion

* A partnership of a gear and a flat, toothed plate
* Converts horizontal movement to rotary motion, or vice versa
* Pulls funicular trains up steep slopes where wheels would slide

What an awesome duo! With us in control, you'll always be heading in the right direction. Circular, toothed Pinion meshes with playmate Rack (like Gear, but with the teeth unwound and laid flat). When Pinion rotates, Rack moves to one side or the other. Together we form the steering system in motor vehicles, allowing the wheel to move the wheels (if you follow).

Rack and Pinion

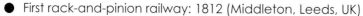

● First rack-and-pinion railway: 1812 (Middleton, Leeds, UK)
● Steepest funicular railway: 48 % (Pilatus Mountain Railway, Switzerland)
● First patent on rack-and-pinion steering: 1975 (Arthur E Bishop, Australia)

✳ Reduces friction in the workings of a machine
✳ Fitted to axles, it allows wheels and gears to move freely
✳ Some of these fluid movers need a bit of lubrication

Bearing

A *smooooth* operator, I make machinery run effortlessly and noiselessly. I may be a strip of metal or plastic sandwiched between two contact surfaces. Or, perhaps, the more fancy ball or caged roller bearings (which work because things roll better than they slide). You'll find me nestling in your bike wheel hubs or killing time (and friction) in your watch to keep it bang on!

● First caged roller bearings: 1740s (John Harrison, UK)
● First patent on ball bearings: 1869 (Jules Suriray, France)
● Jewel bearings: used by watchmakers to reduce energy lost to friction

Lever

■ Movers 'n' Shakers

☀ A simple device for changing the size of a force
☀ Made up of a rigid length and a pivot
☀ Generally grouped in three different classes

Straight as a rod, I'm a pushy so-and-so. I can amplify your effort to give you super-strength or reduce it so that you don't crush itty-bitty things. All you need to get some leverage is a rod and a pivot (called a fulcrum).

With my three classes of lever I can move the Earth! Class one levers, such as a crowbar, place the fulcrum in between your applied force and the thing you want to shift. Even the weediest effort will prise the lid off a can or jemmy open a heavy door in no time. A wheelbarrow is a class two lever, with the fulcrum at one end, your force at the other and the load in between. It makes lifting heavy goods a real doddle. A baseball bat is a class three lever. With the fulcrum at one end and the load at the other, it magnifies your effort to send a ball flying. Wowzer!

● Scissors: a pair of class one levers pivoted around the same fulcrum
● Nutcrackers: a pair of class two levers joined at the fulcrum
● Tweezers: a pair of class three levers joined at the fulcrum

Lever

Pulley

Movers 'n' Shakers

* A clever rope-over-grooved-wheel combo
* Makes light work of hoisting and carrying heavy loads
* Two or more pulleys put together are called block and tackle

Check out my muscle! My smart system of passing a line over a grooved wheel changes the direction of your effort. Pull *down* on my rope and a bucket of water rises *up* out of a well. I'm used for raising flags or closing curtains and, famously, in cranes. With the cable doubled and running over several pulleys, a crane is able to lift stupendous weights. "Groove-y" man!

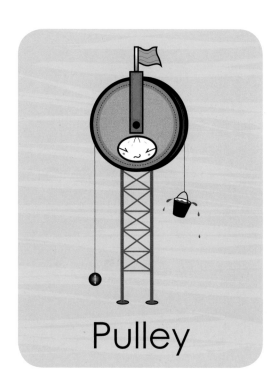

Pulley

● Fixed pulley: only changes the direction of force
● Movable pulley: free to move in space and so gives mechanical advantage
● World's strongest crane: 20,000-tonne capacity (Taisun)

Hydraulics
Movers 'n' Shakers

* This athlete operates on high-pressure fluid power
* Employed to transmit force precisely
* Used for vehicle brake and power-steering systems

Hydraulics

Welcome to the rollickin', *hydraulickin'* world of sealed cylinders, each one a fluid-filled barrel with a piston inside. Press the brake pedal in a car, and you put the fluid on one side of the piston under pressure. The piston moves away to equalize the pressure, while a rod connected to the piston transmits the movement as a forceful push to ja-ja-jam on the brakes.

● Invention of the hydraulic press: 1795 (Joseph Bramah, UK)
● Common applications: bus doors, tipper trucks and arms of diggers
● Largest excavator: 52 m³ bucket capacity (Bucyrus RH400)

Spring
■ Movers 'n' Shakers

☀ This bouncy fella stores mechanical energy when deformed
☀ Perfect for uncoupling vibrations between two objects
☀ Flat and coiled springs are usually made of hardened steel

Howdy! You know me – the dude that makes jumping up and down on the bed soooo much fun! Anything elastic gets to be in my gang – just so long as it gives bounce-back! Say hello to the longbow, wooden springboard and pliers, all just as much springs as my more usual squashy, stretchy, bendy coils of metal.

I come in three main types: compression (squashed short); tension (stretched long); and torsion (tightened in a spiral). It takes energy to squash, stretch or twist me, but do I bend out of shape? No way! I store the effort in my loops and deliver it right back when I spring. I provide the power to keep spring-driven watches going and help machines like click-top pens and brushes in motors maintain tension between parts. Boy, I need to unwind!

● Applications: jack-in-a-box (compression); Slinky (tension); mousetrap (torsion)
● Invention of the innerspring mattress: 1871 (Heinrich Westphal, Germany)
● Hooke's Law: the force a spring exerts is proportional to its change in length

Spring

Control System

Movers 'n' Shakers

☀ Uses system-controlling devices to regulate a machine
☀ Mechanical or electronic action is triggered by feedback
☀ Often used in safety mechanisms or fail-safe devices

I'm the Governor. I crack the whip that gets the Movers 'n' Shakers running like clockwork. They do a good job, but they're not smart – you can't switch off a bouncing fool like Spring! No, most machines combine two or more parts and I monitor and control how they operate.

My genius lies in having two parts – sensor and actuator. The sensor provides information about the output of a machine by measuring properties like light, temperature or pressure. The actuator device alters the operation and may do so by mechanical means (say a rack and pinion or a hydraulic valve), or via an electrical circuit. So when Refrigerator's thermostat senses that the temperature is rising too high, the actuator operates an electrical switch to turn on the compressor. My simple click does the trick!

● First feedback control device: 300 BCE (water clock of Ktesibios, Egypt)
● Bang-bang control: switches abruptly from one state (on) to another (off)
● Examples of a bang-bang control system: refrigerator, domestic heating, kettle

Control System

Chapter 2
House Mates

You rub shoulders with these homebodies every day. They are so much a part of your life that you probably cannot imagine the world without them. With CD and DVD about, you probably don't have much time for fusty old Radio, but don't be fooled. This old-timer has hidden talents, making Television's job possible and doing most of the legwork for hotshot Microwave Oven. Beat that for a technology supposedly on its last legs! Light Bulb lights up your life and Telephone chit-chats away. Refrigerator helps you eat well, while toiler Toilet... well, the less said the better! Face it, House Mates rule – let's find out more.

Radio

 Television

 Light Bulb

 Refrigerator

 Microwave Oven

 Telephone

 Toilet

 Clock

 CD and DVD

Radio
House Mates

✴ This dude excels as a global wireless communicator
✴ Streams electromagnetic waves through the air
✴ Uses a transmitter and receiver to get the message across

When it comes to being connected, there's none like me, baby! Invisible radio waves zap music, news, moving pictures and chat speedily and silently across the globe. You know me best as the receiver of these airwaves – your radio set – but I transmit as well as receive great vibes.

Vibrating radio waves are generated by an electronic circuit (transmitter) and whizz through space, pinging back and forth between satellites. All you need is an aerial: my waves get electrons buzzing in the metal antenna, and this electric current is converted into sound or vision (receiver). Simple telegraph uses Morse code's blips and beeps, but I can be modulated – by a second radio wave, called a carrier (AM/FM on your radio), or digitally – to deliver voice and music. Ah, sweet sounds!

● First working radio: 1894 (Oliver Lodge, UK)
● First transatlantic radio signal: 1901 (Guglielmo Marconi, Italy)
● Speed of radio waves: 299,792,458 m/s (same as speed of light)

Radio

Television
■ House Mates

⁎ A splendiferous moving-picture entertainer
⁎ Uses radio waves to pipe TV shows into your home
⁎ This global channel-hopper is changing to digital transmission

The house entertainer, I'm just bursting with hyperactive, multi-coloured, thousand-watt brightness! I'll tell you what the weather's up to, I'll keep you bang up to date with events, I'll even do a little educatin' while I'm about it!

I use Radio's electromagnetic waves to carry my fab broadcasts. They're transmitted in channels using ultra-high frequencies (UHF). Each channel has two signals – one for pictures and one for sound. When picked up by a receiver (your TV set), Radio's waves convert into electrical signals. These activate a colour grid to make pictures on your screen. Today's plasma, LCD and LED screens use hundreds of thousands of tiny lamps to do this. The picture updates 50 to 60 times a second to give the appearance of movement. Lights, camera... action!

● First demonstration of moving pictures: 1925 (John Logie Baird, UK)
● Number of world's households with at least one TV set: 1.2 billion
● TV frequency band: 470 to 854 MHz

Television

Light Bulb
■ House Mates

☀ One of the world's most important innovations
☀ This bright spark radically changed the lives of our ancestors
☀ Incandescent light bulbs waste electrical energy as heat

I am totally switched on – inventing me was such a bright idea! Of all the House Mates, I've had the single greatest impact on people's lives. Before me, lighting up after dark was messy – much better to hit the sack at nightfall.

With me in your house you can stay up late. I make the streets safer after dark and double the working day for manufacturers! An early version of me is the incandescent bulb. A thin metal wire sits within my glass body and glows white-hot when an electric current passes through it. I'm filled with an unreactive gas, such as argon, to stop it catching fire. But that's not so *bright* after all! I only convert ten per cent of the energy into light. My newer, fluorescent lamps use five times less energy and last about ten times longer. Light fantastic!

● First light bulb patent: 1841 (Frederick de Moleyns, UK)
● Energy conversion of an incandescent bulb: 90 % (heat); 10 % (light)
● Energy conversion of a compact fluorescent lamp: 30 % (heat); 70 % (light)

Light Bulb

Refrigerator
■ House Mates

✳ This cool operator uses a simple heat pump for its inner chill
✳ Keeps drinks and food fresh and slows bacterial attack
✳ A freezer works on the same principle, but at a colder setting

The k-k-king of cool, you'll find me chillin' in the kitchen, stuffed full of lovely munchies. A real hit with the whole family, I keep food fresh for much longer, allowing you all to have a yummy balanced diet.

Do you hear my motor running? That's my compressor hard at work moving heat from my insides to the outside. It works by compressing a special gas until it becomes a liquid. This is then pumped inside me where it turns back into gas, taking heat with it, just like evaporating sweat cools your forehead. Back outside, the gas is compressed again and a metal grid radiator helps me lose the heat to the air (which is why I am always hot round the back). When the fluid returns to room temperature it is compressed and the cycle begins again. No sweat!

● Invention of the first practical fridge: 1876 (Carl von Linde, Germany)
● Optimum fridge temperature: 3 to 5 °C
● Before the invention of the fridge, cold salt water was used as a refrigerant

Refrigerator

Microwave Oven
■ House Mates

☀ This speedy whizz knows all there is to know about *fast* food
☀ Uses energetic radio waves to heat up your meals
☀ The food is heated internally so it does not brown

Hungry and in a hurry? Well, look no further! I cook with lightning speed, taking food from frozen to fiery in a flash. I'm the king of the reheat and the prince of popcorn!

I use a device called a magnetron to generate high-frequency radio waves. They are channelled into my oven and scattered by a rotating fan. These microwaves are absorbed by water, fat and sugar molecules in food, making them rotate in the changing electric field. The more the molecules vibrate, the hotter the food becomes. My design means I can't help setting up hot spots of concentrated radio waves, so I have a rotating carousel to make sure I cook evenly. Put a plate of marshmallows on a non-spinning piece of cardboard and you'll see these hot spots magically appear. Spooky!

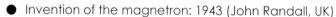

● Invention of the magnetron: 1943 (John Randall, UK)
● First commercial microwave oven: 1954
● Microwave frequency: 2.45 GHz

Microwave Oven

Telephone
■ House Mates

* ☀ Telecoms device that transmits encoded sound as electricity
* ☀ Lets you tell someone you love them when they are far away
* ☀ Hooks up the planet's nations to help them do business

Yakety-yak! I'm a chatty chappy who likes to bring people together. I've made the world smaller by letting folk talk to one another when they are apart.

When you pick up my handset, a local exchange powers it up, connects a digit-receiving device to the line and produces a dial tone to tell you that I'm ready. The exchange decodes the number you punch in and sends a pulsed signal if the line is free (*ring, ring*). Picking my partner up at the other end completes the circuit and you can shoot the breeze for as long as you like! My circuitry converts your natter into electrical signals that are carried on copper wires from your home. Fibre-optic Cable helps to carry data from local exchanges, while Radio sends international calls via Satellite. Zappety-zap!

* ● First patented: 1876 (Alexander Graham Bell, USA)
* ● First coast-to-coast telephone call in the USA: 1915
* ● First pay phone created: 1889 (William Gray, USA)

Telephone

Toilet
■ House Mates

☀ Teams up with sewers to make our lives cleaner
☀ Some public WCs feature infrared-controlled automatic flushing
☀ Dry toilets and dual flushes are green innovations

I'm an unassuming chap and yet I am put upon and sat upon all the time. I'm the stalwart that carries your mess away, keeping the bathroom, street and neighbourhood smelling sweet. It's a dirty job but someone has to do it. I do it very well, as it happens, and I'm *flushed* with pride!

Everyone needs to go at some point and I'm always there when you need me. I come in many types, from sit-down throne to the squat, to tiny aircraft lavs and the space-age, self-cleaning "turdis". Most flushing toilets use a system popularized by Victorian plumber Mr Thomas Crapper. The handle opens a valve, releasing water from the cistern into the pan. A floating ballcock controls the water level in the cistern, triggering a tap when it falls and closing it off when it is full. Ready when you are!

● First flushing system: 1596 (John Harington, UK)
● Average cistern capacity of a modern toilet: 6 litres
● Estimated world population without access to a proper toilet: 2.6 billion

Toilet

Clock

■ House Mates

☀ This steady character always makes a timely appearance
☀ Operates using a mechanism called an oscillator
☀ The more accurate the oscillator, the more precise the clock

Tick. Tock. Can't. Stop. A stickler for punctuality, I keep the world ticking over. I like everything to run on time. Oh yes, without me there'd be chaos, I tell you. Chaos!

My many forms work using the same basic components. The key is my oscillator – a mechanism that produces regularly spaced pulses. In mechanical timepieces this may be a pendulum, while electronic clocks have a vibrating quartz crystal. The oscillator is kept going by a power source, such as gravity, a spring, batteries, mains electricity. Oscillators produce many pulses per second, some more than 32,000, so a mechanism for counting one pulse a second is needed. Gears do this in a mechanical watch. And then comes the best bit! An indicator (my beautiful face) tells you what the time is!

● First mechanical clock: 1088 (Song Dynasty water clock, China)
● First digital clock: 1968 (Peter Petrov, USA)
● Most reliable: NIST quantum logic clock (accurate to 1 sec in 3.7 billion years)

Clock

CD and DVD
■ House Mates

☀ These party starters are big on the digital data storage scene
☀ Consist of a layer of aluminium sandwiched between plastic
☀ Each of them is read optically using a laser

Introducing... the sound and vision duo! Man, we bring the party! The premier mode of data storage, you'll find us packing music, movies, games and so much more.

CD started the revolution by converting sound waves into digital code – gone are those scratchy analogue formats, tape and vinyl. And what CD did for sound, DVD did for vision. Both work the same way: a layer of polycarbonate plastic is etched with pits in a spiral from centre to outer edge. The pattern of pits contains the data. On top of this goes a shiny layer of aluminium and a protective lacquer. When a laser is shined up through the polycarbonate and bounced off the aluminium, an electrical signal is generated by the changes in reflectivity caused by the pits. Starting to get the picture?

● CD: Compact Disc; DVD: Digital Versatile Disc
● First music album released on CD: 1982 (52nd Street, Billy Joel)
● First film released on DVD: 1997 (Twister)

CD and DVD

Chapter 3
Mega Materials

Wow! This lot are ace-in-the-hole magicians with a host of tricks up their sleeves. The Mega Materials are the stuff that many things are made of, and their properties are what make them so important. Strength, hardness, being waterproof or flexible – each of these guys has one or more amazing characteristic that makes it suitable for particular uses. There's no point in making a car out of wobbly silica jelly! The magic lies in taking raw materials – the stuff we find in and on the Earth – in their natural states, and turning them into useful substances. Well, this lot are just right for the job. C'mon! Let's find out what they do.

Paper

Concrete

Steel

Plastic

Ceramics

Fertilizer

Explosives

Smart Materials

Paper
Mega Materials

* A thin sheet used for writing on, wrapping up, even as food
* Made in a paper mill out of a mesh of tiny cellulose fibres
* Comes mostly from softwood trees, such as spruce and pine

I am a starchy original. For centuries people have come to me in search of knowledge. Books, newspapers and letters may be the greatest of my incarnations, but I also make banknotes, as well as tissue, loo and tracing paper.

I'm one of the great inventions of ancient China. "Wood" you believe I get made from mashed-up trees? Under a microscope you'll see my interlocking cellulose fibres. This stuff builds the woody parts of trees and helps them stay upright. I'm made by pulping the wood before cooking it with acid to break down the cells. I'm dyed and put onto rollers where I'm heated, vacuum-dried and compressed to the right thickness before emerging as a big roll, ready for cutting. Textiles are used to make paper money in much the same way – from rags to riches, you might say!

● Most common use: packaging (41 % of all paper used)
● Number of newspapers from an average tree: about 800
● Amount of paper recycled per year in the USA: 41 million metric tonnes (2010)

Paper

Concrete

■ Mega Materials

☀ Hard-nut composite material invented by the Romans
☀ This cement-aggregate mix solidifies when added to water
☀ Hardens over years by reacting with carbon dioxide in the air

I'm a mixing marvel. I may not be cheerful (especially in the rain), but I am certainly cheap, and that has made me the planet's most popular building material. Together with Steel, I have built the modern world – bridges, roads, skyscrapers, dams, pipes, even ships. All me, me, me!

I'm easily stirred up! You just need cement, gravel, sand and water to make a sloppy mixture that stays liquid for a while (if kept moving), but begins to set hard once it settles. It can even set under water, which is why I can be used for bridges and dams. Once poured and agitated to drive off bubbles, I can take several days to harden completely. I'm very good at being squashed, but not so tough if you stretch me. Thankfully, Steel steps in with an internal skeleton to help build up my strength.

● Largest unsupported concrete dome: 43.3 m high (Pantheon of Rome, Italy)
● Invention of modern concrete: 1756 (John Smeaton, UK)
● Invention of reinforced concrete: 1849 (Joseph Monier, France)

Concrete

Steel
Mega Materials

* Hard-as-nails alloy made from iron mixed with a little carbon
* Popular since iron is the cheapest metal to mine and extract
* Combines with hardy concrete to build skyscrapers

A mighty, heighty tower of strength, I build the world's tallest buildings. A thousand times stronger than pure iron, I'm used for everything from cars to cutlery, trains and tools, knives, office blocks and pylons.

I am made in a Bessemer furnace, where molten iron is blasted with oxygen to remove impurities such as sulphur and phosphorus. Modern furnaces convert a staggering 318 tonnes of iron into steel in less than half an hour. Imagine that! A low carbon content makes me tough but easily shaped, while a higher carbon content makes me harder and more brittle. I am further enhanced with the addition of other elements. Chromium prevents me rusting, while manganese makes me super-tough enough for use in rails and rock crushers. Grrr – I am the Man of Steel!

● Typical carbon content (by weight): 1.2 to 2 %
● Amount of steel made per year: 1.3 billion tonnes
● World's tallest steel-framed building: 828 m (Burj Khalifa, Dubai)

Steel

Plastic
Mega Materials

* Modern material made from plants or refined crude oil
* Classed as thermosoftening plastics and thermosetting plastics
* Cheap, mouldable and very durable, with multiple uses

I am one bright and cheery dude, with an amazing ability to mould to any shape. My many forms are made from polymers – atoms joined together in long, flexible chains. Most are hydrocarbon chains with additives that determine colour, hardness, flexibility or weight. Get me!

Thermosetting plastics are moulded when hot and stay in shape when they cool, even if heated again. With thermosoftening plastics, however, the polymers can slide over each other and be remoulded every time they are heated. I really get about. I make the cases for electrical gizmos and home appliances and am used in the construction trade. You'll find me in cars, planes and boats, fabrics, toys and packaging. But I tend to hang around and have got a bad rep for pollution. Shame!

● First man-made plastic: 1856 (Parkesine, Alexander Parkes, UK)
● Amount of plastic rubbish in the oceans: 17,000 pieces per square kilometre
● Average lifespan of a plastic bottle: 300 to 500 years

Plastic

Ceramics
Mega Materials

- A hard and brittle gang made of nonmetallic crystals
- Moulded into shape and then fired hard with heat
- Range from old-school pottery to high-tech materials

Ancient in origin, we have stood the test of time. We are smooth, glassy and cold – hard enough to stop a bullet, resistant to chemical attack and impervious to heat.

Sounds impressive? Well, there's more! Unlike many materials, we refuse to be bent and built upon and are simply too hard to be cut or shaped. While tough when compressed, we're brittle and shatter easily. Because of this, we each tend to be cast as a single piece – a perfect one-off. The first ceramic materials were clay, which contains kaolinite minerals. Today's advanced ceramics use crystals of silicon carbide, zinc oxide, zirconia and silicon nitride. These make fantastically hardwearing parts that have many uses from car disc brakes to bulletproof vests. It's perfectly "potty"!

- Temperature range for firing ceramics: 1000 to 1600 °C
- Common ancient uses: pots, tiles, tableware and decorative figures
- Modern-day uses: blades, turbine rotors, insulators, bearings, semiconductors

Ceramics

Fertilizer
Mega Materials

* This farming favourite makes barren land fertile
* Allows the ground to be used year after year without a break
* Promotes copious growth of roots, leaves, shoots and flowers

Oooh! I love to feel the soil between my toes. Spread over fields, I put back into the earth the elements that growing plants take out. Without me the land wouldn't support decent crops for long. But don't mess with me. Used too much, I make soil too acidic to grow plants and cause algal blooms in waterways that use up all the oxygen and stifle life. You have been warned!

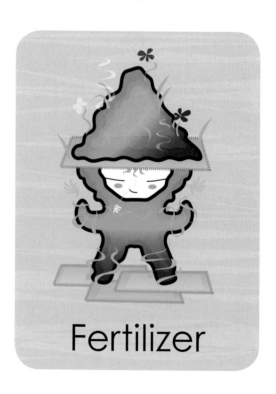

Fertilizer

● First factory-made fertilizer: 1842 (superphosphate, UK)
● Organic fertilizers: horse manure, guano (seabird dung), powdered limestone
● Inorganic fertilizers: ammonia, phosphate pentoxide (from rock phosphorus)

Explosives

Mega Materials

* ✹ Materials that cause rapid and violent chemical reactions
* ✹ Release energy as pressure, sound, heat and light
* ✹ Useful for blasting rocks to reveal Earth's riches

Explosives

Living life on the edge, we have a nasty habit of going off with a BANG! Our destructive power comes from the energy stored in our chemical bonds. Many of us are based on elements that join together very tightly – nitrogen, carbon and oxygen. When their bonds break, they release their energy very quickly, in a rush of expanding gases and heat. It's a blast!

- ● Invention of gunpowder: 9th century BCE (China)
- ● Detonation speeds of commercial explosives: 1800 to 8000 m/s
- ● Largest (non-nuclear) explosion: 6 kilotons of TNT (N1 rocket launch, 1969, USSR)

Smart Materials
Mega Materials

* Visionary types that respond to changing conditions
* Some claim to have self-healing properties
* Further development of these smarties will change the world

A bunch of new materials containing whizzo particles, we are real smart cookies. Compared to our meagre Mega Materials pals, we're far out. We are the future, my friend!

We are able to change in appearance, behaviour or shape according to conditions around us – temperature, stress, electric and magnetic fields, or acidity, say. Many of our applications are futuristic, but you may know some of us already. One of our gang includes voltage-sensitive (electrochromic) material in LCDs that changes the colour and transparency of Television's screen. Sharp, eh? Then there are shape-memory alloys that *remember* the form of your specs, even if you squash 'em. Some day, toilet seats will warm up when you sit on them and your car will be able to change colour to suit your mood!

● Photomechanical materials respond to a change in light conditions
● Piezoelectric materials change size with electricity
● Halochromic materials respond to a change in acidity

Smart Materials

Chapter 4
Groovy Gizmos

This crew are micro-sized prizefighters who punch well above their weight. Because they have slotted so comfortably into everyday life, it's easy to overlook just how much of a shake-up these Groovy Gizmos have caused. These heroes sparked the digital revolution – a method of encoding and manipulating information that has led to an incredible explosion of technology. Digital devices deal with information as strings of ones and zeros that are really electrical pulses – "on" (1) and "off" (0). None do this better than mighty Microchip, a string-puller extraordinaire. It's time to find out why.

Microchip

Mobile Phone

Computer

User Interface

Digital Camera

Flash Memory

Microchip
Groovy Gizmos

* Semiconducting electronic circuit found in all electronic gizmos
* A billion transistors can fit on a thumbnail-sized microchip
* This mini genius is also known as an integrated circuit

Get *me*! I am the master of all gadgetry, the crux at the core of all electronic devices. My mini circuits are shrunk onto tiny slabs of silicon and built up into eye-wateringly complex combinations of components.

I'm a diddy fella but, boy, do I pack a punch. I call the shots inside your laptop, your mobile phone, MP3 player and games console. Without me, those Gizmos have no groove! I reduce every request to a sequence of simple sums and logic operations. The secret of my genius lies in the transistor – basically, a switch that is controlled by the state of other switches. When current passes through a transistor, we say its state is 1, otherwise the state is 0. These 1s and 0s are bits. And the binary code of bits is the basis of all operations. That's pretty special, right?

- Typical transistor density: 1 million transistors per square mm
- A byte: a sequence of eight bits
- A nibble: half a byte

Microchip

Mobile Phone
Groovy Gizmos

※ Roaming communications device using a network of cells
※ Holds personal and security details on a removable SIM card
※ Has changed society and revolutionized life in far-off places

I'm a free-range bird, I simply love to roam. Thanks to me you can keep in touch with your mates when you're on the go. It's a very *moving* thought!

I provide a service that allows you to make calls or send texts and I use Radio's waves to zap them through space. Highly charged Battery powers me up and User Interface helps push the right buttons. Coverage comes via a network of cells, each with a mast in the centre. When you make a call, I find the mast with the strongest signal and communicate with it. Each cell operates on its own frequency and my clever circuitry handles the complex business of switching frequencies as you move between cells. I do it seamlessly, without losing the signal. Not a word is lost, so you never notice it happening!

● SIM: subscriber identity module
● World's first call made from a cellular phone: 1973 (USA)
● First phone-to-phone SMS (short message service) text message: 1993 (Finland)

Mobile Phone

Computer
Groovy Gizmos

✸ This electronic whizz-kid stores and processes all kinds of data
✸ Uses a programmable silicon chip called a microprocessor
✸ Reduces all instructions to simple sums and logic operations

I am the superbrain of this Gizmo groove. Quick thinking and logical to the core, I control the systems that make trains run on time, I operate shop tills, design books, add special effects to movies and fly planes without the pilot!

I have a user interface, some memory and – brain of the superbrain – a central processing unit (CPU) that can be programmed to do almost anything. It can crank out a massive 150,000 million instructions a second! A control unit within the CPU handles the order in which tasks are done, sending and retrieving the results from a block of temporary random-access memory (RAM). A hard disk stores your software, an optical drive reads and writes CDs and DVDs, and a video card processes information for displaying on a screen. Now that's brain power!

● First computer built: 1938 (Z1, Konrad Zuse, Germany)
● First microprocessor chip issued: 1973 (Intel 4004, USA)
● Moore's Law: the number of transistors on a microchip doubles every two years

Computer

User Interface
Groovy Gizmos

* Helpful device that allows control of an electronic machine
* A typical input device is a mouse, keyboard or touchscreen
* Can also use speech or facial expression recognition

A Groovy Gizmo go-between, I let you talk to computers. Don't let my highfalutin name scare you. "Interface" just means to "be in touch", and "User" – well, that's you, pal!

I'm all about input and output. An input device feeds instructions to a computer, and the computer uses an output device to give a response. Take a pocket calculator. You input the workings of a sum by punching the keys on the number pad. Hidden from you, the onboard processor calculates the answer, then it displays it on the screen in numbers you can understand. Most input devices use simple prods and pokes (think mouse or keyboard). Outputs are most often visual – a screen or read-out, even the dials of a car dashboard or that light flashing red on the power station control panel... yikes!

● First graphical user interface developed: 1981 (Xerox Star, USA)
● Gorilla arm: the pain caused by operating vertically mounted touchscreens
● Electronic-paper (e-paper) display: Amazon Kindle (2007, USA)

User Interface

Digital Camera
Groovy Gizmos

- Computer-operated camera that creates digital files
- Uses a microchip to convert light into binary code
- Allows live events and news to reach you in record time

I spy with my digital eye and, boy, what I can see! I'm one versatile dude, finding my way into mobile phones, laptops and telescopes, on the tips of medical probes, even on board interplanetary spacecraft.

I store images as digital files, which means I can display them instantly on an LCD screen – no fussy negatives or chemicals here! Pictures are easily edited, cropped and retouched, before being pinged by email, posted on the internet or sent via deep-space radio link. My genius lies in a very special microchip called a charge-coupled device (CCD). When photons (particles) of light hit tiny cells on my chip's grid, the light energy is converted into electricity. The chip counts the electrical charge per cell to assess how bright each area of the image should be.

- Invention of CCD: 1969 (Willard Boyle and George Smith, USA)
- Pixel count: refers to the number of cells on a CCD chip
- Common picture file formats: JPEG and TIFF

Digital Camera

Flash Memory
Groovy Gizmos

* Lightweight, portable memory used in electronic gizmos
* This upstart has shaken things up in the world of data storage
* Also known as solid-state memory

Whizz, flash, bang! I'm a wizard for compact handiness. Every memory card or stick has my chips nestling inside. I'm used in flash drives, tablet PCs and slot memory cards – I've even been used in space exploration robots.

I am one hundred per cent electronic, have no moving parts and do not require power to save information. This makes my memory "stable" or "non-volatile". It's a trick that allows me to retain stored data even when the computer is switched off, or when your flash memory card is rattling about in your pocket. It also makes me ideal for storing the information that your computer needs to boot up and get running in the first place. Central to my workings is a rewritable flash memory chip, which allows you to add and remove data, quite literally, in a flash!

* Invention of flash memory: 1980 (Dr Fujio Masuoka, Japan)
* First Memory Stick launched: 1988 (Sony, Japan)
* A USB connector provides power and a data channel for flash drives

Flash Memory

Chapter 5
Super-tech Crew

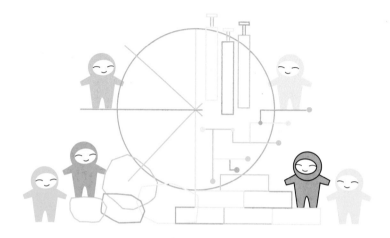

The Super-techs count among the most advanced machines on our planet, each one a leader in its field. Internet, Fibre-optic Cable and Satellite have changed the way we communicate and access data. They have altered life on Earth way beyond our wildest imagination. Wireless Communication and Smart Card have made life on the move simplicity itself, while Spacesuit allows humans to survive the hostile conditions of outer space. Particle Accelerator, the world's largest machine, seeks the smallest parts of matter, while Robot's potential grows by the day. Let's hear what they have to say...

Radar

Satellite

Laser

Fibre-optic
Cable

Wireless
Communication

Internet

Barcode

Smart Card

Printing Press

3D Printer

Spacesuit

Robot

Particle
Accelerator

Radar

Super-tech Crew

* Technology that detects objects, using radio waves
* Uses "echolocation", a trick borrowed from whales and bats
* Uses include defence, astronomy and weather forecasting

What ho! I'm a proper wartime hero, a real dish! I was invented in the 1930s, to warn of approaching enemy aircraft, and I remain dedicated to keeping people safe.

I scan the sky with pulses of Radio's clever airwaves. They bounce off any object they hit, pinging a small portion of them back towards my receiving antenna. This allows me to calculate the exact location, direction and speed of anything out there. Only the most modern stealth technology escapes detection. Today, I have a truly diverse range of applications. I help sea captains detect the shoreline and other ships, while air traffic control uses me to stack airliners in the sky to avoid collisions. I locate anything from fast-moving missiles to gathering weather formations. In fact, I think I detect a spot of rain coming!

● First radar: 1934 (Sir Robert Watson-Watt, UK)
● Originally an acronym, RADAR stands for RAdio Detection And Ranging
● First radar speed gun: 1954 (Bryce K. Brown, USA)

Radar

Satellite
■ Super-tech Crew

☀ Computer-controlled device orbiting planet Earth
☀ Mainly solar powered, but many also have onboard batteries
☀ Used for weather-watching, navigation, spying and research

Peer up into the night sky some time and you might see me. I look just like a star, but gaze for long enough and you'll see that I am on the move, silently circling Earth.

I am blasted into orbit on board Rocket and spat out at speeds reaching 27,000 km/h. Once in space, I control my flight path, power consumption and temperature automatically. I am not alone out here – there are hundreds of us! Weather satellites pass over Earth's poles once every 100 minutes. GPS satellites circle the planet twice a day at 20,350 km, while communications satellites as high as 35,786 km stay in one position above the surface, rotating in tandem with Earth. But nothing lasts forever: once defunct we move to a graveyard orbit, adding to the 25,000 bits of junk that litter space.

● First satellite launched: 1957 (Sputnik 1, Russia)
● Most satellites are in low Earth orbit, between 160 and 2000 km above Earth
● GPS: Global Positioning System, used for map-making and navigation

Satellite

Laser
■ Super-tech Crew

☀ Produces monochromatic, coherent and focused light
☀ Achieves visible, infrared and ultraviolet frequencies of light
☀ Great for removing embarrassing tattoos and unwanted hair!

Zap! Pow! I'm razor-sharp, a vision of the future. Some say I am a little humdrum, what with barcode readers and printers everywhere. But my industrial lasers and scalpels offer the very latest in *cutting-edge* technology.

Unlike the light produced by Light Bulb, mine is strictly a single frequency, which means I produce one colour only. My light rays are rigidly organized, too, with all the photons in step with each other. This is why I make direct beams, instead of spreading out. I am created inside a lasing medium, which can be solid crystals, semiconductors or gases. The medium is pumped with electricity to excite it into producing light, and there I am! Scientists at the US National Ignition Facility are trying to use me to create nuclear fusion. Now that *is* the future!

● Number of laser beams at NIF: 192
● Temperatures reached at NIF: almost 50 million °C
● LASER stands for Light Amplification by the Stimulated Emission of Radiation

Laser

Fibre-optic Cable
■ Super-tech Crew

☀ Pipe that carries pulses of light by "total internal reflection"
☀ Uses include transmission of internet and telephone data
☀ Also used in surgical equipment, to bring light inside the body

The big chief of data transmission, I take the lead in global communications. My ultra-thin glass fibres carry pulses of light thousands of kilometres under the ocean.

I am built with a transparent layer of cladding wrapped around a central core. The boundary between the layers acts like a mirror, reflecting light when it hits the sides. This effect bounces light down the tube, guiding waves as they travel along my length. Flashy Laser zaps down my pipes, usually at infrared frequencies. Each pulse is part of a coded stream carrying information – a voice on the telephone or data via the internet, say. Several streams use the same pipe on different light frequencies, allowing each of my cables an impressively huge bandwidth (capacity). Well, I've always been a big band fan!

● Typical number of fibres in a cable: 1000
● Optical cables transmit data at 182,000 km/s
● Data rate record: 155 channels, at 100 Gb/s, over 7000 km (Bell Labs, France)

Fibre-optic Cable

Wireless Communication

Super-tech Crew

- ☀ A conjuror that gives radio-linked access to the internet
- ☀ Better known as Wi-Fi and Bluetooth
- ☀ Bluetooth transmits data on 79 fast-changing radio bands

Look, no wires! With my incomprehensible powers I allow electronic devices to talk to each other *with no physical connection*. Spooky, huh? Not really – your machine just needs a built-in wireless adapter to make it happen.

I use Radio's waves to send messages to a base station as Wi-Fi. This wireless access point provides a gateway to the internet, through which any wireless-enabled Gizmo can enter. Meanwhile Bluetooth unites electronic devices, allowing them to share info – swapping files on two phones, for example. Unfortunately, Microwave Oven and cordless Telephone use the same frequency band and can cause interference. *Ring, ring*. Ping!

- ● Range of Wi-Fi: 20 m (indoors)
- ● Range of Bluetooth: 5 to 10 m
- ● Wi-Fi distance record: 420 km (Swedish Space Agency)

Wireless
Communication

Internet
■ Super-tech Crew

☀ A vast network of interconnected computers
☀ Sends requested information as "packets" of data
☀ The World Wide Web is just one of many internet services

The world's biggest computer network, I am a real know-it-all. I am bulging with useful info and pictures of cute pets. My wires zing with emailers, tweeters and bloggers, buyers and sellers, file sharers and personal bankers.

Don't confuse me with the World Wide Web. Oh no, I am the whole shebang – the physical bits of kit that make up the global system. I fill warehouses and take the energy of 40 power stations to run. Every device connected to my system has an internet protocol (IP) address through which it can send and receive packets of data. Each time you access a large server (think Google) you view files on its hard drive. These are sent to your computer in small data packets and my routers (handling millions per second) have to direct each one to the right computer!

● Invention of the internet: 1962 (J C R Licklider, USA)
● First packet-switching network established: 1969 (ARPANET, USA)
● Number of spam messages received each day: 200 billion

Internet

Barcode
■ Super-tech Crew

✳ A printed code made from solid bars and gaps
✳ Commercial products carry a universal product code (UPC)
✳ UPCs help keep track of stocktaking for shops and businesses

Looking for me? Take a look at the back cover of this wonderful book, dear reader. My classic form is a series of vertical bars whose width and spacing represent a neat, unique, machine-readable number. On commercial goods this is generally an item code. Read by a laser scanner, I've made supermarket checkouts swift and trouble-free (well, almost).

Barcode

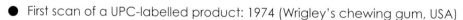

● First scan of a UPC-labelled product: 1974 (Wrigley's chewing gum, USA)
● Introduction of the barcoded airline boarding pass: 2005
● Quick Response (QR): 2D code designed for reading by smartphones

Smart Card
Super-tech Crew

* Clever critter, aka a chip card or integrated circuit card
* Plastic card with a tiny microprocessor chip embedded in it
* This pocket-sized safe pair of hands is a mine of information

Smart Card

Do not fear, I am here! A mighty protector, I use tiny Microchip to keep all your data secure. I'm used for storing security details on bank cards and medical records on health cards, I can be a driver's licence, an identity card, even Mobile Phone's precious SIM card. How? Well, a card reader connects to my fancy gold-plated contact pads to operate Microchip, and I reveal all!

● Data reading rate: 106 to 848 kilobits per second
● Size of contact area: 1 cm^2
● Contactless card: operates using radio frequency identification (RFID)

Printing Press

■ Super-tech Crew

☀ The traditional method used for making printed pages
☀ A highly significant invention for the spread of ideas
☀ The Chinese invented the technique over 1000 years ago

An oldie but a goldie, some hail me as the single most influential invention ever! Just think of the newspapers printed every day; all the books in schools, libraries and shops; this book in your hands. It's certainly im-"press"-ive!

Early versions of me were large wooden screw presses that knocked out 250 pages an hour. They pushed an inked plate on to a blank sheet of paper to make an imprint. Thanks to the development of movable type, pages were assembled more quickly by slotting letters, punctuation marks and spaces into a grid. Modern-day offset-printing presses are two-storey juggernauts churning out 50,000 pages an hour! Colour is made by printing on four different colour plates.* It's an expensive business so let's hope there are no mistaykes!**

● Invention of the printing press: around 1440 (Johannes Gutenberg, Germany)
● *Cyan, magenta, yellow and black (CMYK)
● ** There's one right there!

Printing Press

3D Printer
Super-tech Crew

☀ Up-and-coming technology that builds stuff in one piece
☀ This click-and-print marvel is ideal for making custom-made items
☀ Pieces are made of just one material, so recycling is easy

I'm the one to watch. A superstar in the making, I can create 3D shapes by "printing" them – layer upon thin layer of material – until a solid object emerges.

I'm currently used to make prototypes of manufactured products, but soon I will be producing almost anything you need, right there in your home. Toys, toolboxes and tables, chairs, cutlery and coat hangers: if you can draw it, I can print it! (And if you can't draw it, don't worry, Internet will have designs you can download.) I use two processes: direct printing and laser sintering. In the first, I spray a fine film of plastic polymers or thick wax, using inkjet nozzles like those in a 2D printer. For laser sintering, I direct powerful ultraviolet lasers to convert liquid plastic into solid shapes. Oh yes, I'm one "form"-idable dude!

● Size of 3D dots: 0.05 to 0.1 mm
● Thickness of layers: about 0.1 mm
● Time it takes to make a plastic 3D printed flute: 15 hours

3D Printer

Spacesuit
■ Super-tech Crew

* ✹ Tough and reliable protection for astronauts
* ✹ More of a one-person spacecraft than a piece of clothing
* ✹ Has legs that are colour-coded to identify the occupier

I'm a cosmic hero, an outer-space lifesaver. Sure, human bodies are fine-tuned to living conditions on Earth, but get them out here and things get very scary... fast!

Going out in space without me is not a good idea! Within minutes, a lack of oxygen knocks you out. You cook in the sunlight (120 °C) and freeze in the shade (–100 °C). The lack of air pressure makes your blood boil, and then there's the radiation... No, you're better off with me. My modules clip together to make a pressurized suit providing oxygen and removing carbon dioxide. My hard, fibreglass torso protects your vital organs and a gold coating on the clear, plastic bubble helmet blocks most radiation. Between my layers runs a web of pipes carrying water, keeping you cool, calm and collected.

* ● Number of parts in a typical spacesuit: about 18,000
* ● Number of separate steps to putting on a spacesuit: 25
* ● Length of pipes in a typical spacesuit: 91.5 m

Spacesuit

Robot
■ Super-tech Crew

※ An automated machine dedicated to a life of service
※ Has a brain, operated by a computer program
※ Can be either self-operating or with some operator control

I'm used like some high-tech Cinderella, doing things that humans find too dull, difficult or dangerous. But I have a brain, you know, and can make decisions for myself.

I mow the lawn, pick fruit, clean out pipelines, sniff out and defuse bombs, help astronauts work in space, find shipwrecks, build cars from scratch, perform keyhole surgery... Phew! I even have my own football teams. Humanoid robots, such as my heroes ASIMO and TOPIO, mimic humans, but it's quite hard to get the mechanics right. It's usually easier not to go on legs, for example, so I often use tracks or rollers. They say a robot is only a robot if it has a brain (although it can also have an operator). But what about a heart? I'd be a faithful companion, we'd be great friends. Whaddya say?

- Leonardo's robot: automaton designed by Leonardo da Vinci, Italy, 1495
- Robots in use today: over 50 % Asia; 32 % Europe; 16 % North America
- Cost of building one ASIMO unit: US $1 million

Robot

Particle Accelerator
■ Super-tech Crew

✳ A machine that is used to break up atoms
✳ Gives subatomic particles energy in the process
✳ The smallest parts of matter hold the deepest secrets

A real smasher, I pump pressure onto matter until it spills the secrets of the Universe. I'm not talking about atoms here. No, no, no, I'm after the very smallest parts in the mix – the so-called hadrons and quarks.

I get my oomph from super-high energies, which help me break up nice, stable atoms that would rather stay whole. From there, it's simple. I use powerful magnets to accelerate the itty-bitty blips to phenomenal speeds and then slam them into one another inside gigantic detectors! Scientists sift through the wreckage to look for evidence of undiscovered new particles. My Large Hadron Collider zaps particles around a 27 km circular track, built 100 m underground. It is colossal equipment for detecting particles smaller than you can imagine!

● Grandfather of modern particle accelerators: Rolf Widerøe, Norway
● World's largest particle accelerator: Large Hadron Collider (LHC), Switzerland
● Particles in the LHC complete the 27 km loop 11,245 times per second

Particle Accelerator

Chapter 6
Petrolheads and Power Freaks

Like you, a machine needs energy to get it moving, and that's a job for this bunch of heavies. The Petrolheads are prime movers – engines that convert energy (often from chemical fuel) into motion. The Power Freaks provide, store and transmit driving force to other machines. But there's a catch! Whether it's the chips you had for lunch or a handful of plutonium rods, all fuels require you to consider how best to use them. Popping out for a carton of milk in the car slurps up the energy it takes to get a tonne of metal rolling down the road – it's probably just as easy to walk, and you might want to work off those chips…

Sail

 Piston Engine

 Jet Engine

 Rotor

 Rocket

 Ion Thruster

 Electric Motor

 Generator

 Battery

 Fuel Cell

 Solar Power

 Nuclear Power

Sail
Petrolheads and Power Freaks

☀ This prime mover harnesses the energy of moving air
☀ Acts like a wing to lift a vessel up, as well as drive it forwards
☀ Used for transport over water, ice, sand and across space

I'm an old sea dog, a hoary explorer who has traversed the oceans on great voyages of discovery. Unfurling to catch the slightest puff of wind, I take advantage of this free source of energy that swirls around the planet.

Meeting the wind head on creates a dead zone that leaves me all out of puff. I go slack and flappy, and can't propel the craft. But by tacking, or zigzagging, I deflect the wind like an aircraft wing, creating a force that pushes the boat forwards. On water, I can go at a fair clip – faster, even, than the wind speed itself – but it's in space that I really make the distance. Using ultra-thin mirrors, I catch the steady stream of particles and radiation coming from the Sun. This solar wind can drive spacecraft at cruise speeds of 70 km/s! Well, blow me!

● Dead zone, aka being "in irons" : 30° to 50° either side of the wind
● Nautical speed: 1 knot = 1.85 km/h
● First solar sail: 2010 (IKAROS – 200 m² and 0.0075 mm thick)

Sail

Piston Engine
Petrolheads and Power Freaks

✳ Drives motor vehicles powered by gasoline or diesel
✳ Has a two-stroke, four-stroke or six-stroke cycle
✳ Generates electricity for those not connected to a power grid

I am the workhorse for motorized transport. Cough, splutter and wheeze I might, but I've been around the block a few times and I'm still firing on all cylinders!

A sturdy old-timer, I house a hollow cylinder with a combustion chamber at the top. I burn fuel in here, triggering an explosion that would blow less hardy types apart! The blast sends a piston hurtling down my cylinder – the first of four down and up strokes that make up one of my cycles. The first (down) sucks in air and fuel, while the next (up) compresses the mix. My spark plug fires and… BOOM! – a power stroke (down) provides the driving force. The final stroke (up) pushes the exhaust out of my belly. To even out my one-power-stroke-every-four motion, I often have several cylinders in the same block.

● Aka internal combustion engine, because it burns its fuel inside the engine
● First successful four-stroke engine: 1876 (Nikolaus August Otto, Germany)
● Average efficiency of a car engine: about 25 %

Piston Engine

Jet Engine
Petrolheads and Power Freaks

* This fly boy powers airliners, fighter planes and speedy autos
* A form of internal combustion engine, aka a gas turbine engine
* Airliners have turbofan engines; fighter jets have turbojets

I'm a speedy high-flyer, who just loves a good blowout! You'll have seen me on an aircraft – slung under the wing or attached to the tail fin – but I also boost powerboats and cars to world speed records. Catch me if you can!

Like wheezing Piston Engine, I burn fuel inside my body, but you won't see me wasting my energy driving pistons! No, I use the force of hot exhaust gases to create thrust. It all starts with whirring fan blades at my front end, which suck air into my combustion chamber and compress it to a tenth of its original volume. Jet fuel is sprayed into the chamber and ignited. The expansion of the exploding mixture sends hot gases screaming out of my rear, and the momentum of this rear-end expulsion creates an equal thrust in the opposite direction. It's a blast!

● First operational jet engine: 1939 (Hans von Ohain, Germany)
● Combustion chamber temperature: 550 to 700 °C
● Land speed record: 1228 km/h (Thrust SSC, UK, 1997; turbofan)

Jet Engine

Rotor
■ Petrolheads and Power Freaks

☀ Horizontally spinning fan that lifts a helicopter into the air
☀ This gyrating Jimmy is driven by a turboshaft jet engine
☀ When spinning vertically, a rotor pulls a craft forwards, not up

I'm a dizzy kinda fella, a real whirlin' dervish. I'm made up of two to five blades that spin round and round at super-high speed to lift things off the ground.

Each of my blades is designed with a curved leading edge that tapers to the rear. Shaped like long, thin wings, they push the air downwards to create a thrust force in the opposite direction (upwards). They can be pitched at a steeper angle to give more lift, or vertically to pull things forward (think propellers). As well as lift, my rotation creates a force that pushes in the opposite direction to that of my spin. This means that most helicopters need an additional rotor on the tail to keep them flying straight. I can do things that an aeroplane can't – I can hover, turn on the spot and fly backwards. Neat, eh?

● First successful helicopter: 1942 (Igor Sikorsky, Russia)
● First turbine-powered helicopter: 1951 (Charles Kaman, USA)
● Tandem-rotor helicopter: powered by two top-mounted rotors

Rotor

Rocket
Petrolheads and Power Freaks

- Works by throwing exhaust gases behind it at high speed
- Carries all necessary fuel and oxidant on board
- Fuel tanks are jettisoned once spent

5... 4... 3... 2... 1... Lift off! Hold on to your hat, baby, as I blast you through Earth's atmosphere and into outer space. I light up the sky as fireworks, missiles, space rockets – and life-saving ejector seats in fighter aircraft.

Like my cousin, Jet Engine, I'm a reaction engine that operates by throwing mass at high speed out of my rear, to produce forward-thrust force in the opposite direction. But in the vacuum of space, there is no air to burn the fuel, so I carry oxygen with me. Take a look at your average spacecraft, and you'll see a number of thin, pencil-like tubes attached to the sides. These carry solid fuel or liquid propellant. They work like fireworks – once lit, there's no going back... Whoosh! Now, that's a reaction I like – c'mon baby, light my fire!

- Speed of exhaust gases at launch: approximately 4.5 km/s
- Escape velocity from Earth: 11.2 km/s
- First rocket in space: 1957 (R-7 ICBM, Russia)

Rocket

Ion Thruster

Petrolheads and Power Freaks

☀ Electric propulsion for interplanetary spacecraft
☀ Reaction engine that uses beams of charged atoms
☀ Silent and more efficient than a rocket engine

I am the Ion Man! I work using the same stuff that makes balloons stick to your hair and cling to jumpers – charged ions. My abilities are simply astronomical!

An ion is an atom with a positive or negative electric charge. Ions with opposite charges attract each other and I take advantage of this. I accelerate ions – positive or negative (I'm not fussed) – towards a metal plate with an unlike, or opposite, charge. These particles pass through holes in the plate to create beams of super-fast ions that can push a spacecraft forwards. While Rocket relies on chucking lots of mass (hot exhaust gases) out behind it, I go for low mass (tiny ions) at blistering speeds. It takes me a long time to get going, but I shift along quietly, building speed as the astro-kilometres flash by.

● First ion thruster mission: 1998 (Deep Space 1, NASA)
● Speed of ion exhaust: 50 km/s
● Tank size: 40 kg xenon tank (GOCE, 2008)

Ion Thruster

Electric Motor
Petrolheads and Power Freaks

* A magical device that converts electric energy into motion
* Harnesses the power of one of nature's fundamental forces
* Small motors power watches; large ones drive ship propellers

I am an electromagnetic wizard! Yes, ladies and gents, before your very eyes I change invisible electricity into motion that pulls, pushes and spins things around. I may seem commonplace – I open windows in cars, drill holes in walls and spin discs in DVD players – but think again!

I rely on the incredible phenomenon that a wire carrying an electric current generates its own magnetic field around itself. Make a loop of this wire and you have an electromagnet. Stick the loop next to a second magnet and it attracts to the magnet's opposite pole: a force is generated. If the current travelling through the wire loop reverses direction every half-turn, the magnetic poles flip and the wire loop spins like crazy. Connect the loop to an axle and, voila, you reap the force – instant power!

● Discovery of principle: 1821 (Michael Faraday, UK)
● First practicable electrical motor: 1888 (Nikola Tesla, USA)
● The smallest electric motor is made of a single molecule

Electric Motor

Generator
Petrolheads and Power Freaks

※ The booming workhorse of the industrial world
※ Converts mechanical energy into electrical energy
※ Power stations use steam turbines to drive their generators

A "gen"-uine power freak, I operate in reverse to that awful boaster, Electric Motor. Extraordinarily powerful, I convert all kinds of mechanical energy into wonderful, tremendously useful electricity. I rule the industrial world!

You can see me in action as the dynamo that powers the lights on your bike, but mostly I toil away in the turbine halls of power stations, heroically providing your house, the streets and all industries with electrical power. I use an energy source to spin a coil of wire inside a magnetic field, and this sparks up an electric current in the conducting wires. I'm so versatile that I can convert pedal power and tidal power into electricity, as well as that from internal combustion engines, steam turbines, water turbines and wind-driven turbines. All power to me!

● World's most powerful generator: 700,000 kW (Three Gorges Dam, China)
● World's most efficient gas turbine: 60 % (Irsching, Germany)
● World's largest wind turbine: 126m rotors (Enercon E-126, Germany)

Generator

Battery
Petrolheads and Power Freaks

✳ Converts stored chemical energy into electricity
✳ Replaced or recharged once chemical reserves are spent
✳ Potentially toxic, used batteries must be disposed of safely

I'm a portable prince, the pocket whizz-kid that runs your wristwatch, calculator and mobile phone. Hook me up to an electrical circuit, and a chemical reaction releases electrons from my negative end, which travel around the circuit to my positive end. These moving electrons create an electric current that powers the equipment attached to it. Simple!

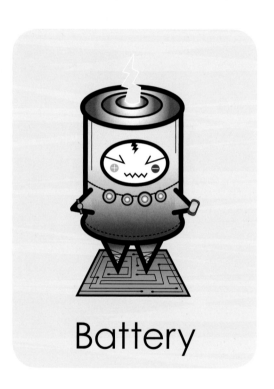

Battery

● First battery: 1800 (Alessandro Volta, Italy)
● Cathode: a battery's positive terminal
● Anode: a battery's negative terminal

Fuel Cell

Petrolheads and Power Freaks

* A special kind of battery powered by hydrogen
* Converts chemical energy in fuel into electricity
* Heralds clean power for cars, buses, boats and submarines

Fuel Cell

I am the green dream. Hug a tree? Man, I love the whole planet! Unlike short-lived Battery, I sup a continuous supply of hydrogen from a tank and take oxygen from the air to power electrical systems. My only other output is water vapour. While that pollutin' Piston Engine chugs away, I run cars cleanly and quietly – a breath of fresh air for a sweeter-smelling future!

- First fuel cell: 1839 (William Grove, UK)
- Efficiency of fuel-cell vehicles: 42 to 53 % (at full power)
- World's largest fuel-cell power plant: 45 MW (Hwaseong City, South Korea)

Solar Power
Petrolheads and Power Freaks

☀ This hot shot converts energy from the Sun into electricity
☀ Earth has an average 12 hours free light and heat each day
☀ Works best in desert areas with little cloud

A little ray of sunshine, I exploit Earth's "stellar" energy source. Every day the Sun bathes our planet in a steady stream of light and heat. Our hot friend provides nearly enough energy in one hour to meet the world's needs for a whole year! I help collect it and convert it to electricity.

I have two ways of doing this – with photovoltaic solar cells and in heat engines. Solar cells are semiconducting silicon chips that emit electrons when they are hit by photons of light. Laid out on solar panels, these sunny-side-up marvels can generate electricity for your home. In heat engines, accumulators and mirrors concentrate the Sun's energy to produce steam that can power booming Generator. These solar furnaces can reach temperatures of up to 3500 °C – hot stuff, indeed!

● Highest altitude for solar-electric aircraft: 29,524 m (*Helios*, 2001, NASA)
● Discovery of photovoltaic effect: 1839 (Alexandre-Edmond Becquerel, France)
● Amount of sunlight absorbed: 19 % (atmosphere); 35 % (reflected by clouds)

Solar Power

Nuclear Power
Petrolheads and Power Freaks

* Converts the energy stored in an atomic nucleus
* Uranium-235 is nuclear fission's most commonly used fuel
* Powers nuclear submarines, warships and some spacecraft

I may start small but don't be fooled. Compared to other fuels, I am super-charged. I give millions of times more energy than the same volume of oil. I'm an atomic hero!

I access the energy residing at the very heart of matter itself. The nuclei of some heavy, unstable elements split when bombarded by subatomic neutron particles (that's some very small particles indeed). And in splitting, they release a huge amount of energy. This process is called nuclear fission and the energy is used to generate electricity in power stations and propel nuclear craft. Sadly, with such awesome power comes great responsibility. The fission process also produces radioactive waste that remains lethally dangerous for tens of thousands of years. I'm hazardous, so please take care.

● First nuclear reactor built: 1942 (Chicago Pile-1, Manhattan Project, USA)
● Proportion of world's electrical energy that is nuclear: 13 to 14 %
● Half-life of iodine-129 (long-lasting nuclear waste): 15.7 million years

Nuclear Power

Index

Glossary

Accumulator A device that stores energy, such as a rechargeable battery.

Additive A way of manufacturing products by building up layers, adding one on top of the next, the opposite of manufacturing objects by removing material.

Alloy A metal blended with other metals or non-metals, to make a material with desirable properties. Alloys include bronze, solder and steel.

Analogue When an electric signal has the same shape as the voice or picture being transmitted.

Atom A tiny particle of matter, made of protons, neutrons and electrons; the smallest component that can take part in a chemical reaction.

Cellulose A material made from the cell walls of green plants and useful in making paper and fabrics, often obtained from wood pulp or cotton.

Digital When an electric signal is a sequence of binary numbers; each number is equal to the size of the voice or picture being transmitted at that moment.

Dynamo Another word for a generator – a machine that turns motion into electrical energy.

Electric charge A property of matter that makes charged particles feel a force when they come close to one another. The two types of electric charge – positive and negative – make electricity possible.

Electromagnetism A fundamental force of nature between electrically charged particles.

Electron A tiny, subatomic, negatively charged particle that orbits around the nucleus of an atom.

Element A chemically pure substance, consisting of atoms of only one type.

Frequency The rate at which something repeats itself; the number of cycles it makes per unit of time.

Friction A force that slows things down or resists forward movement, often by surfaces rubbing together; also called drag.

Hadron Tiny particles of matter made of quarks bound together. Protons and neutrons are types of hadron.

Infrared Frequencies of electromagnetic radiation just below that of visible light.

Magnetic field Produced by moving charged particles, changing electric fields or the spinning electrons of a magnetic material. It generates a force felt by charged objects and other magnets.

Mechanical advantage The measure of how much a tool or a machine boosts force.

Nuclear Anything relating to the nucleus (core) of an atom. Nuclear fusion is the joining together of atomic nuclei and nuclear fission is the process of breaking a nucleus apart.

Glossary

Nucleus The central parts of an atom, made up of subatomic particles called protons and neutrons.

Oxidant Essential to combustion (burning) reactions, an oxidant combines with fuel to produce heat and light energy.

Particle Often called 'subatomic particle', one of the minute parts of matter that group together to make up an atom. All atoms are made of protons, neutrons and electrons.

Photon A particle of light radiation or electromagnetic radiation. It has no mass and no charge.

Photovoltaic The production of electricity by light.

Quark The smallest kind of subatomic particle.

Radioactive An unstable substance, whose atomic nuclei break down and release nuclear radiation.

Semiconductor A material that conducts electricity better than an insulator, but not as well as a metal (conductor). These materials are used to control electric current and are the 'brains' inside all electronic devices.

Silicon A semiconducting element and the base material for microchips.

Subatomic particle Any part of matter that is smaller than an atom.

Transmission The gearbox of a car. It transmits power from an engine to the wheels.

Ultraviolet Frequencies of electromagnetic radiation above that of visible light.